LET'S
see

Halloween

by Natalie M. Rosinsky

Content Adviser: Dr. Alexa Sandmann, Professor of Literacy,
The University of Toledo; Member, National Council for the Social Studies

Reading Adviser: Dr. Linda D. Labbo, Department of Reading Education,
College of Education, The University of Georgia

**Let's See Library
Compass Point Books
Minneapolis, Minnesota**

Compass Point Books
3722 West 50th Street, #115
Minneapolis, MN 55410

Visit Compass Point Books on the Internet at www.compasspointbooks.com or e-mail your request to custserv@compasspointbooks.com

Cover: Halloween jack-o'-lanterns

Photographs ©: Photo Network/Henryk T. Kaiser, cover, 12; Unicorn Stock Photos/Tom McCarthy, 4; North Wind Picture Archives, 6, 10; Mark E. Gibson/Visuals Unlimited, 8; Comstock, 14; Matthew Klein/Corbis, 16; Unicorn Stock Photos/Aneal Vohra, 18; Liba Taylor/Corbis, 20; John Cross/The Free Press, 24.

Editor: Catherine Neitge
Photo Researcher: Svetlana Zhurkina
Photo Selector: Catherine Neitge
Designer: Melissa Voda

Library of Congress Cataloging-in-Publication Data
Rosinsky, Natalie M. (Natalie Myra)
    Halloween / by Natalie M. Rosinsky; reading adviser, Linda D. Labbo.
      v. cm.—(Let's see library)
    Includes bibliographical references and index.
    Contents: What is Halloween?—How did Halloween begin?—Why are ghosts part of Halloween?—Why are witches part of Halloween?—Why are some creatures part of Halloween?—What are other signs of Halloween?—How has Halloween changed?—How is Halloween observed in the United States?—How is Halloween observed around the world?
    ISBN 0-7565-0392-2 (hardcover)
    1. Halloween—Juvenile literature. [1. Halloween. 2. Holidays.] I. Title. II. Series.
    GT4965 .R67 2002
    396.2646—dc21
                                                               2002003043

© 2003 by Compass Point Books
All rights reserved. No part of this book may be reproduced without written permission from the publisher. The publisher takes no responsibility for the use of any of the materials or methods described in this book, nor for the products thereof. Printed in the United States of America.

Table of Contents

What Is Halloween? 5
How Did Halloween Begin? 7
Why Are Ghosts Part of Halloween? 9
Why Are Witches Part of Halloween? 11
Why Are Some Creatures Part of Halloween? 13
What Are Other Symbols of Halloween? 15
How Has Halloween Changed? 17
How Is Halloween Observed in the United States? 19
How Is Halloween Observed Around the World? 21
Glossary 22
Did You Know? 22
Want to Know More? 23
Index 24

4

What Is Halloween?

Let's pretend. There are monsters in the dark! Scream and shiver. Wear a mask and have fun! These are **customs** some people observe every October 31. This evening is Halloween.

Halloween combines different beliefs. Long ago, the fearful **Celts** prayed to their god of the dead. They believed that good and evil spirits were near. The Celts were happy, too. Their **harvest** was done. The ancient **Romans** also had feasts then. They prayed for their dead and to their harvest goddess.

◀ *Masks and costumes are part of Halloween.*

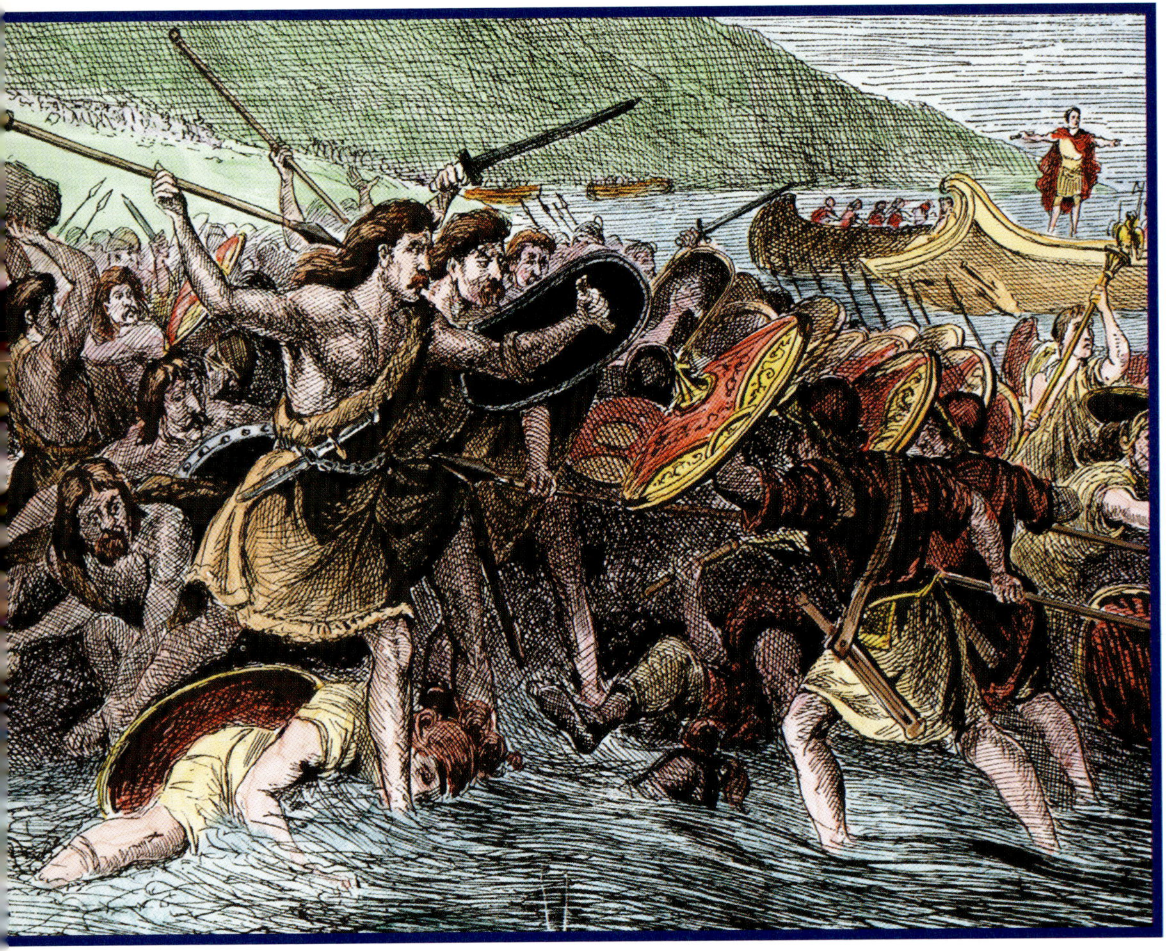

How Did Halloween Begin?

When the Roman army beat the Celts, their customs combined. Later, Rome accepted **Christianity**. Christian leaders made old Celtic and Roman customs into new Christian ones.

Bonfires were once lighted against evil spirits. Now, they kept away the devil. People had prayed for their dead. Now, Christians prayed for those who had died for Christianity. This happened on November 1. It was called All Saints' Day or All Hallows' Day. The evening before was called All Hallows' Even. This was October 31. People shortened this name to Halloween.

◄ *The Roman army fought the Celts and others.*

8

Why Are Ghosts Part of Halloween?

Later, another Christian holiday began. All the dead were remembered on All Souls' Day, November 2.

Food was set out to help friendly spirits. Maybe it would also keep evil spirits happy! Wandering spirits or ghosts had been old Celtic and Roman ideas. Now they were Christian ideas. An Irishman named Jack was said to be one such ghost. "Jack's lantern" came to be called a jack-o'-lantern. It was used to scare other spirits. A lamp was made by lighting a candle inside a carved turnip. Later, pumpkins were used instead.

◀ *Jack-o'-lanterns decorate a porch at Halloween.*

10

Why Are Witches Part of Halloween?

Some women knew how to heal sick people with plants. Sometimes, this knowledge was feared. Christian leaders believed these women might really work for the devil!

These wise women were hunted as witches. Hundreds of thousands were killed. People feared witches as though they were evil spirits. The spirits were said to wander on Halloween. People felt most afraid of witches then.

People thought witches dressed in black and flew on broomsticks. By the 1800s, this idea was part of Halloween.

◀ *Many women, including this one on trial, were accused of being witches in Salem, Massachusetts, in the late 1600s.*

12

Why Are Some Creatures Part of Halloween?

People believed that witches used creatures for their evil magic. Some ancient people had prayed to cat goddesses. Black cats became feared at Halloween. People thought they helped witches.

How could flying bats see in the dark? This mystery made people fear the small, winged creatures. Hooting owls seemed able to turn their heads around. Bumpy toads were able to swell in size. People feared these creatures, too.

◀ *A black cat is a Halloween symbol.*

14

What Are Other Symbols of Halloween?

Halloween colors are black and orange for several reasons. Witches wore black. Dangerous cats were black. Bonfires and jack-o'-lanterns blazed orange. A popular harvest food, the pumpkin, was orange.

Other **symbols** of Halloween come from the past. People thought that spirits took shape as trolls or other monsters. They thought ghosts could rise from graves.

Perhaps a grinning jack-o'-lantern could keep away these evils. Maybe wearing a mask or costume would hide someone from these monsters.

◀ It's fun to wear black and orange costumes on Halloween.

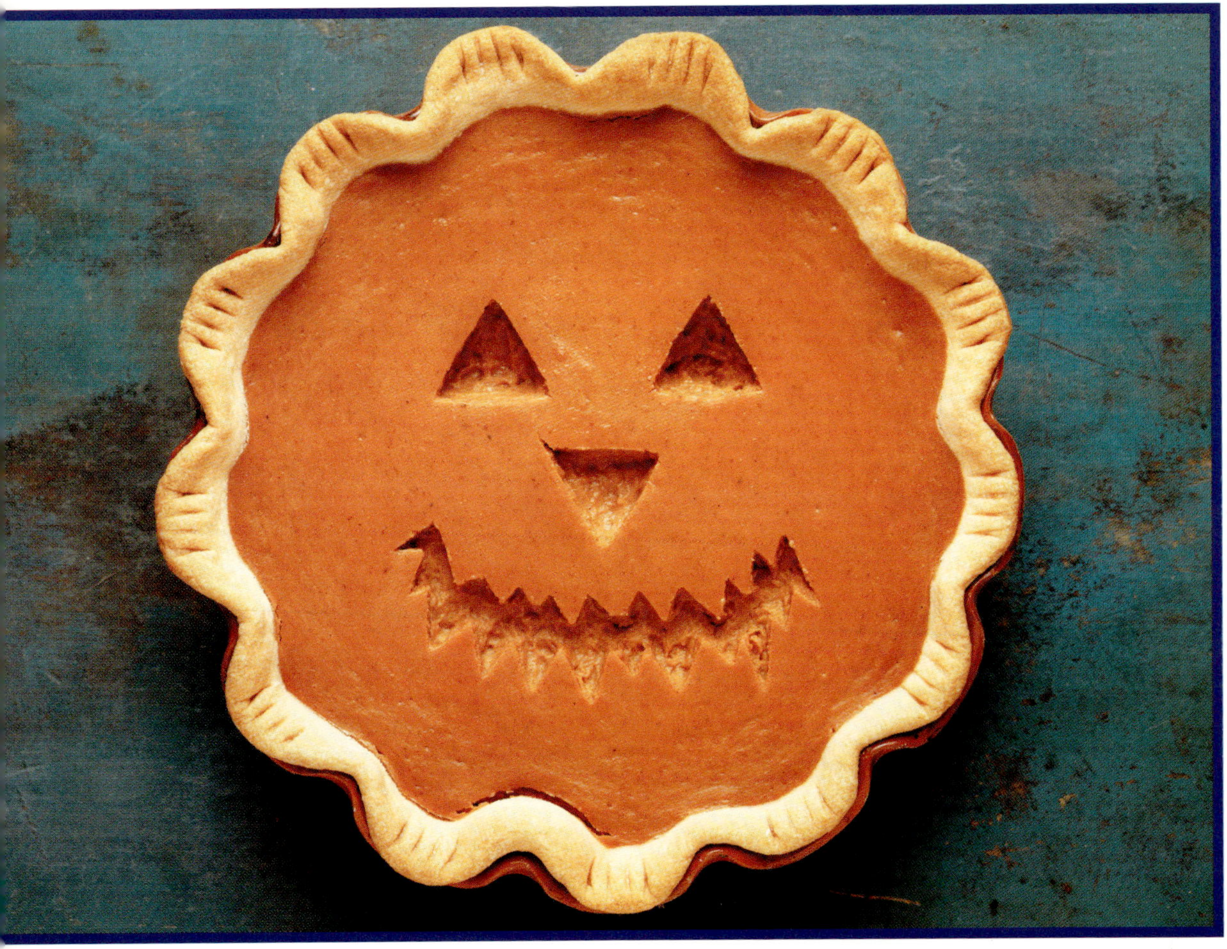

How Has Halloween Changed?

Halloween was once called "Snap Apple Night" or "Nut Crack Night." One **superstition** was about apple peels. A long peel tossed over a woman's shoulder was important. It was supposed to show the name of the man she would marry!

Harvest foods are still popular. People enjoy apples and nuts. Pumpkin pie tastes great! People no longer believe that foods can show what will happen.

Today, most people do not believe in evil spirits or ghosts. They are not really afraid at Halloween.

◄ *A pumpkin pie is made to look like a smiling jack-o'-lantern.*

18

How Is Halloween Observed in the United States?

People from Ireland and Great Britain brought Halloween to America. It became a widespread custom in the 1840s. Halloween is not a national holiday. Schools, businesses, and government offices are open on Halloween.

On All Souls' Day, children had asked for pennies or cakes. People had worn masks and costumes to trick evil spirits. These customs became Halloween trick-or-treating.

Other customs are hayrides, haunted houses, and parties. Making jack-o'-lanterns and decorating for Halloween are also fun!

◀ *Children wear costumes to Halloween parties.*

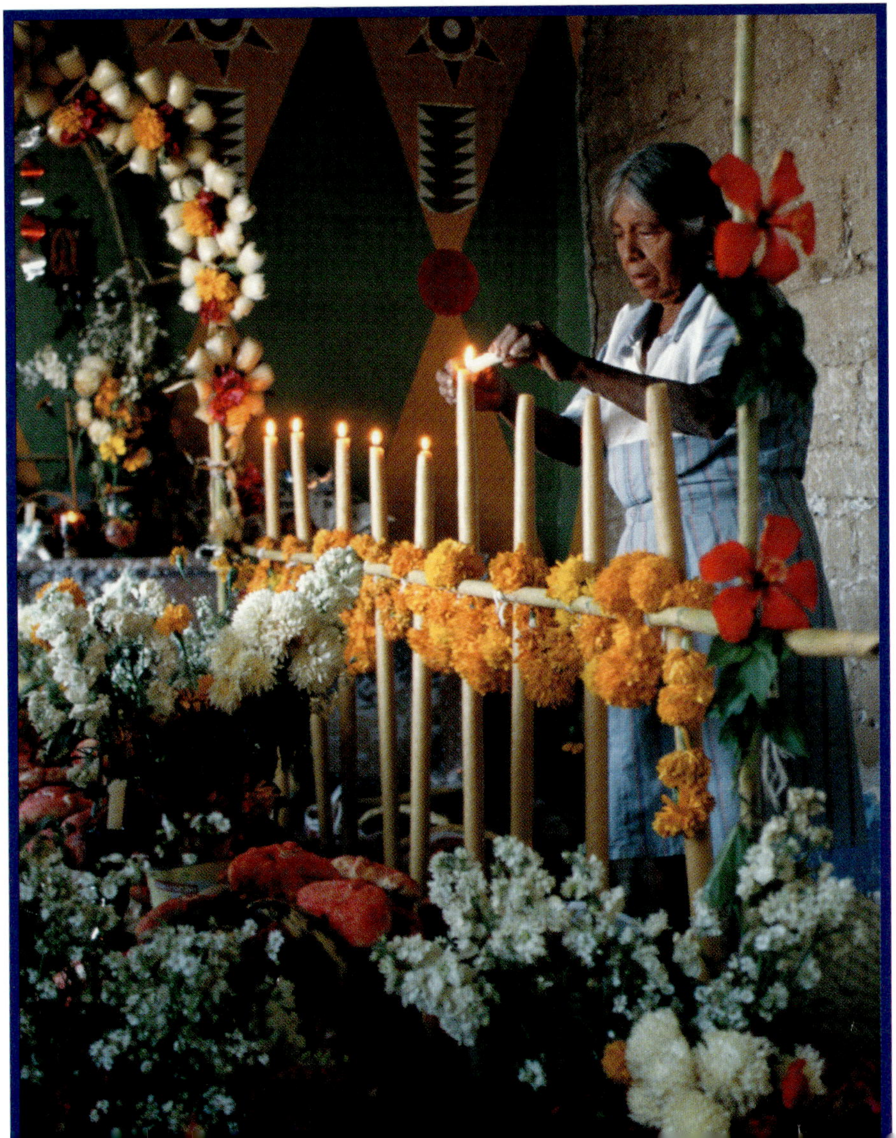

How Is Halloween Observed Around the World?

In Canada and Ireland, children also trick-or-treat, wear costumes, and have parties. Some Irish superstitions remain. Find the ring baked into a cake, and you will soon marry!

In France, All Saints' Day and All Souls' Day are legal holidays. People visit family graves then. Families gather to remember their dead.

In Mexico and Spain, Halloween begins a happy holiday called the Day of the Dead. Families welcome and honor the souls of their dead. Mexican-Americans may also observe this day.

◄ *A Mexican woman lights candles to honor her dead family members on the Day of the Dead.*

Glossary

Christianity—the faith that believes Jesus Christ is the son of God
customs—things regularly done by a group of people
Celts—people who long ago lived in Ireland, England, Scotland, Wales, and France
harvest—gathering in of a crop when it is ripe
Romans—people who came from Rome, a city that long ago governed many lands
superstition—a foolish belief based on fear and the unknown
symbol—something that represents something else

Did You Know?

- The word "Halloween" was first used in the 1500s.
- The Irish used turnips and beets to make their jack-o'-lanterns. The custom of using pumpkins began in the United States.
- The largest jack-o'-lantern in the world was carved from an 827-pound (375-kilogram) pumpkin in California.

Want to Know More?

In the Library
Barth, Edna. *Jack O' Lantern*. New York: The Seabury Press, 1974.
Black, Nola. *Creepy Crawly Critters and Other Halloween Tongue Twisters*. New York: HarperCollins, 1995.
Hoyt-Goldsmith, Diane. *Day of the Dead: A Mexican-American Celebration*. New York: Holiday House, 1994

On the Web
13 Pumpkin Avenue
http://www.hometown.aol.com/pumpkinave/
For Halloween crafts, crossword puzzles, jokes, recipes, music, and more

Not Just for Kids! Halloween Tricks and Treats
http://www.night.net/halloween/
For Halloween music, stories, crafts, and recipes

Through the Mail
UNICEF (United Nations International Children's Emergency Fund)
Dept. 3064P
P.O. Box 98006
Washington, DC 200090-8006
To learn how you and your friends can help children around the world while you have holiday fun. Since 1950, children in the United State have collected $110 million to help others!

On the Road
Salem Witch Museum
Washington Square
Salem, MA 01970
978/744-1692
To learn more about so-called witches in the American colonies. The city of Salem also has Halloween activities throughout October.

Index

All Hallows' Day, 7
All Hallows' Even, 7
All Saints' Day, 7, 21
All Souls' Day, 9, 19, 21
bats, 13
black cats, 13, 15
bonfires, 7, 15
cats, 13, 15
Celts, 5, 7
Christianity, 7, 11
colors, 15
costumes, 15, 19, 21
customs, 5, 19

Day of the Dead, 21
foods, 9, 15, 17
harvest, 5
jack-o'-lanterns, 9, 15, 19
owls, 13
pumpkin pie, 17
pumpkins, 9, 15
Romans, 5, 7
superstition, 17
toads, 13
trick-or-treating, 19, 21
witches, 11, 13, 15

About the Author
Natalie M. Rosinsky writes about history, science, and other fun things. One of her two cats usually sits on her computer as she works in Mankato, Minnesota. Both cats pay close attention as she and her family make and eat special holiday foods. Natalie earned graduate degrees from the University of Wisconsin and has been a high school and college teacher.